FORGIVENESS

Making Peace with the Past

8 STUDIES FOR INDIVIDUALS OR GROUPS

LifeGuide®
BIBLE STUDIES

DOUGLAS CONNELLY

IVP Connect

An imprint of InterVarsity Press
Downers Grove, Illinois

InterVarsity Press
P.O. Box 1400, Downers Grove, IL 60515-1426
ivpress.com
email@ivpress.com

InterVarsity Press® is the book-publishing division of InterVarsity Christian Fellowship/USA®, a
movement of students and faculty active on campus at hundreds of universities, colleges and schools of
nursing in the United States of America, and a member movement of the International Fellowship of
Evangelical Students. For information about local and regional activities, visit intervarsity.org.

LifeGuide® is a registered trademark of InterVarsity Christian Fellowship.

Cover image: © Tony Garcia / Getty Images

ISBN 978-0-8308-3094-7

Printed in the United States of America ∞

g green press INITIATIVE As a member of the Green Press Initiative, InterVarsity Press is committed to protecting the
environment and to the responsible use of natural resources. To learn more, visit
greenpressinitiative.org.

| P | 31 | 30 | 29 | 28 | 27 | 26 | 25 | 24 | 23 | 22 | 21 | 20 | 19 | 18 | 17 | 16 | 15 | 14 |
| Y | 34 | 33 | 32 | 31 | 30 | 29 | 28 | 27 | 26 | 25 | 24 | 23 | 22 | 21 | 20 | 19 | 18 | 17 |

Contents

Getting the Most Out of *Forgiveness*

Forgiveness is a choice. It's choosing to absorb the hurt. It's paying the debt ourselves. It's extending grace to someone who deserves the opposite.

Forgiveness is also a door to peace and joy. But it's a small door, and it can't be entered without stooping—or kneeling. Sometimes, the door of forgiveness is very hard to find.

The truth is we all need to be forgiven. The Bible makes it painfully clear that every one of us has built up an enormous debt of sin to God. The payment of that debt required nothing less than the sacrifice of God's own Son, Jesus. The Father is now free to forgive us. Someone else has paid the penalty we deserve.

Christians rejoice in the forgiveness we receive from God, but the rub comes from other people. When we hurt the people we love, how do we go about restoring the relationship? When we suffer the pain of betrayal or injury or rejection from someone else, how do we deal with the anger and resentment we feel? This study guide will help us find some answers.

The answers we discover won't be easy answers. Living out God's truth will require a great deal of courage and humility. But if we will follow Jesus in learning to extend grace, if we will cultivate a forgiving spirit, we will find a greater sense of peace and freedom than we have ever known before.

This study guide follows two themes—God's forgiveness of us and our forgiveness of others. Begin at the place where you sense the greatest need in your own life. Then move to the other studies. As you understand more about God's gracious forgiveness of you, your own capacity to forgive will be expanded and strengthened.

So bring your broken heart, your shattered dreams, your desires for revenge, your guilt and shame. Let God transform life's worst experiences and your deepest failures into a powerful witness of his grace and love.

Suggestions for Individual Study

1. As you begin each study, pray that God will speak to you through his Word.

2. Read the introduction to the study and respond to the personal reflection question or exercise. This is designed to help you focus on God and on the theme of the study.

3. Each study deals with a particular passage—so that you can delve into the author's meaning in that context. Read and reread the passage to be studied. The questions are written using the language of the New International Version, so you may wish to use that version of the Bible. The New Revised Standard Version is also recommended.

4. This is an inductive Bible study, designed to help you discover for yourself what Scripture is saying. The study includes three types of questions. *Observation* questions ask about the basic facts: who, what, when, where and how. *Interpretation* questions delve into the meaning of the passage. *Application* questions help you discover the implications of the text for growing in Christ. These three keys unlock the treasures of Scripture.

Write your answers to the questions in the spaces provided or in a personal journal. Writing can bring clarity and deeper understanding of yourself and of God's Word.

5. It might be good to have a Bible dictionary handy. Use it to look up any unfamiliar words, names or places.

6. Use the prayer suggestion to guide you in thanking God for what you have learned and to pray about the applications that have come to mind.

7. You may want to go on to the suggestion under "Now or Later," or you may want to use that idea for your next study.

Suggestions for Members of a Group Study

1. Come to the study prepared. Follow the suggestions for individual study mentioned above. You will find that careful preparation will greatly enrich your time spent in group discussion.

2. Be willing to participate in the discussion. The leader of your group will not be lecturing. Instead, he or she will be encouraging the members of the group to discuss what they have learned. The leader will be asking the questions that are found in this guide.

3. Stick to the topic being discussed. Your answers should be based on the verses which are the focus of the discussion and not on outside authorities such as commentaries or speakers. These studies focus on a particular passage of Scripture. Only rarely should you refer to other portions of the Bible. This allows for everyone to participate in in-depth study on equal ground.

4. Be sensitive to the other members of the group. Listen attentively when they describe what they have learned. You may be surprised by their insights! Each question assumes a variety of answers. Many questions do not have "right" answers, particularly questions that aim at meaning or application. Instead the questions push us to explore the passage more thoroughly.

When possible, link what you say to the comments of others. Also, be affirming whenever you can. This will encourage some of the more hesitant members of the group to participate.

5. Be careful not to dominate the discussion. We are sometimes so eager to express our thoughts that we leave too little opportunity for others to respond. By all means participate! But allow others to also.

6. Expect God to teach you through the passage being discussed and through the other members of the group. Pray that you will have an enjoyable and profitable time together, but also that as a result of the study you will find ways that you can take action individually and/or as a group.

7. Remember that anything said in the group is considered confidential and should not be discussed outside the group unless specific permission is given to do so.

8. If you are the group leader, you will find additional suggestions at the back of the guide.

1

Our Forgiving Father

Luke 15:11-32

Every evening the old man sat on the porch after a hard day of work. He looked out the gate and down the road, hoping to catch a glimpse of a traveler. During the day, out in the fields, he would stretch his back and scan the horizon, watching for a figure headed home.

Then one day he saw him. A thin, ragged young man turned in from the road, and the father knew it was the person he had been waiting for. In a burst of joy and desperate anticipation, the old man did something his servants had never seen him do. He *ran* to meet his son.

GROUP DISCUSSION. Did you ever run away from home? Where did you go, and what happened?

PERSONAL REFLECTION. Who is the "obedient" one in your family or among your friends? Who is the wild one? How do they get along?

Jesus' story of the prodigal son never fails to move our hearts with joy and relief. We come empty and broken to God, and he makes us his own dear children. Even though we've squandered his gifts and ignored his wishes, he runs to welcome us home. *Read Luke 15:11-32.*

---

1. Based on what you have read and on your own experience, how would you describe the younger son's feelings when he first left his father's home?

when he was living it up in a distant land?

when he was feeding pigs?

when he saw his father running toward him?

---

2. Which stages in the younger son's journey parallel stages in your life? Explain the similarities.

---

3. Do you think the father was wise in giving the younger son his part of the inheritance to begin with? Why or why not?

4. Why did the father stay at home and wait for the son's return instead of going out to find the son?

5. What other ways could the father have responded to the returning son?

6. Using the father's welcome of the runaway son as the pattern, what would you tell someone about God's response to the sinner who returns to him?

7. What do you think the younger son's attitude and behavior toward the father was after his return?

What does that tell you about the Christian's motivation to live obediently to God?

8. What do you find in the older brother's response that is reasonable and understandable?

How does the father respond to the older brother's objections?

_____

9. Do you identify more closely with the younger brother or the older brother in the story? Explain why.

_____

10. Based on the father's words to both brothers in this parable, what personal words would God say to you if he sat down with you and had a father-to-child talk?

Ask God to help you take his words of instruction and insight to heart.

Now or Later

Jesus actually told three linked parables on this occasion. What does the story of the lost sheep (Luke 15:3-7) and the story of the lost coin (Luke 15:8-10) reveal to you about God's character?

What "undeserving" person can you demonstrate God's love and grace to this week?

How will you do it?

2

Why We Need Forgiveness

Ephesians 2:1-10

We were practicing the most intense part of the Easter musical. The drama team and the musical team joined their voices together to clamor for Jesus to be crucified. The shouts and noise echoed over and over through the church auditorium. When we stopped for a break, I was surprised to see the man behind me crying. He was an elder in the church and mature in the Lord, but tears streamed down his face. "I can hear myself shouting," he sobbed. "If I had been there, I would have screamed for Jesus to die too!"

GROUP DISCUSSION. Think of the most evil person you have ever encountered or heard about. Do you think you would be capable of committing the same crimes or not? Explain your answer.

PERSONAL REFLECTION. Contemplate the worst thoughts that have ever crossed your mind. Where did those evil thoughts come from?

The decision to forgive another person does not arise from sheer willpower. The most compelling source of strength is always our own need—our own sense of failure and our own experience of God's forgiveness. The apostle Paul gives us a very focused picture on how far from God we once were and how powerfully God worked to rescue us. *Read Ephesians 2:1-10.*

1. Based on this passage, how would you describe the spiritual condition of a person who has never believed in Christ?

How have you seen this to be true in your experience with other people?

2. What marks us out as sinners—our outward behavior or our inner nature? Support your view from verses 1-3.

3. Forgiveness emerges from three aspects of God's nature—his love, his mercy and his grace. Explain each quality in your own words.

4. How can we demonstrate God's character toward people who wrong us?

_____

5. According to verses 4-6, what has happened to the inner nature of the person who believes in Jesus?

_____

6. How does it make you feel when you think about your condition before you believed and then when you think about what you have received by God's grace?

_____

7. What would you say to a person who is trusting in religious activity or good works to get God's approval (vv. 8-9)?

_____

8. What response does God require of us in order to receive his forgiveness?

9. What insight does that give you regarding how we are to forgive others?

10. Throughout this passage, God assures us of his willingness to forgive those who believe in him. What can we do to assure other people of our willingness to forgive?

Ask God to help you remember that you were once lost and separated from him—and that in grace and love you were found.

Now or Later

Verse 10 explains the role of good works in a Christian's life. We do not do good works in order to be made right with God; we do good works because we have been changed by God's power. New behavior flows from a changed heart. Forgiven people forgive. What good work for God can you do this week? Tell someone else (perhaps in your small group) what you intend to do, and ask them to hold you accountable to do it.

3

Confessing Our Sin

When I was fifteen, a friend and I decided to camp out overnight in his backyard. About 1:00 a.m. we left the backyard and went on a small-scale vandalism rampage in our town. We left a trail of flat tires, broken light bulbs and overturned flowerpots. The next day the police showed up and gave our parents a full report. My friend's father blew it off as a childish prank; my father took a different approach.

He drove me to each place we had been the night before, and I had to talk to each homeowner or business owner. My dad didn't confess for me; I confessed. I also offered to pay for or work to repair any damage I had done. I couldn't make excuses or blame other people. I had to face everyone I had wronged and admit what I had done.

GROUP DISCUSSION. Do you have a hard time admitting when you are wrong, or do you "confess" to more than you are guilty of? Tell a story from your life that illustrates your answer.

PERSONAL REFLECTION. Think about a time when you tried to hide sin or wrong. How did it feel (or how might it feel) to be able to confess it fully.

Some pretty weird ideas are floating around about how we should deal with sin and failure in our lives and about how we receive God's forgiveness. Some of those same ideas were around even in the early years of the church. The apostle John writes this passage to set the record straight about sin and forgiveness in a Christian's life. *Read 1 John 1:5—2:2.*

1. What do you envision about God when you read: "God is light; in him there is no darkness at all" (1:5)?

Why do you think the message that God is light is such an important message for Christians to hear?

2. What does it mean then to "walk in the light" (1:7)?

3. What mistaken view about lifestyle and about relationship with God does John expose in 1 John 1:6? Explain it in your own words.

4. If we walk in the light, why do we need to rely on the blood of Jesus to purify us from all sin?

5. If we are purified from all sin, how should we respond to feelings of guilt?

6. How do some people deceive themselves according to 1 John 1:8?

Why does John later write that he wants Christians not to sin (2:1)?

7. The word *confess* means "to say the same thing." We confess sin when we say the same thing about our sin that God says about it. Using that insight, how would you direct a younger Christian to confess a sin to God?

8. *God's promise of forgiveness rests on God's faithful character. He consistently responds to confession in the same way. How does that truth give you assurance when you confess?*

9. The goal of the Christian is to live without sin (2:1). What promise can we claim when we fail to reach that goal (2:1-2)?

10. What would you say to a person who says, "It doesn't matter how I live because God will forgive me"?

How would you respond to a person who says, "I've sinned too deeply for God to forgive me"?

Praise Jesus for being your atoning sacrifice on the cross—and your defense lawyer every day.

Now or Later

James encourages us to confess our sins to each other (James 5:16). Who would you feel safe "confessing" to? In what ways might confession to another person help us? Ask God to lead you to an accountability partner who will help you grow as a Christian. If you already have an accountability partner or group, ask God to strengthen those relationships and deepen those commitments.

4

The Shout of a Forgiven Man

Psalm 32

Corrie ten Boom's story of forgiveness has been read by millions of Christians. Corrie and her sister, Betsie, were sent to a Nazi prison camp in 1943. Their crime was harboring Jews in their Dutch home. At the Ravensbruck prison camp, Corrie's sister died.

A few years after the war, at a church service, Corrie came face to face with one of the guards from that camp. The man came up to Corrie after her message and told her how grateful he was for her words. "To think that, as you say, God has washed my sins away," he said.

The man's hand was extended, but Corrie struggled to move her hand from her side. Her silent prayer mingled with the feelings of revenge in her heart: "Jesus, I cannot forgive him. Give me your forgiveness."

Corrie's testimony is that, when she took her former jailer's hand, love for the man sprang into her heart. The healing of the world, she concludes, hinges not on our forgiveness but on God's.*

GROUP DISCUSSION. Think about your various groups of friends—neighbors, colleagues, church members. What responses do you think your various friends would suggest to Corrie as she faced the former prison guard?

What emotions would you have struggled with in the same situation?

PERSONAL REFLECTION. How do you picture God's face when you come to him with a request? What expression does he wear when you have done something wrong?

Psalm 32 emerged from another well-known story of forgiveness. Israel's King David had pursued a sexual encounter with another man's wife. When she became pregnant, David had arranged for the other man to be killed in battle. Eventually, God exposed the whole story. In response to David's confession, God forgave David's sin. Psalm 32 is David's joyful expression of freedom and gratitude to God for his grace and cleansing. *Read Psalm 32.*

---

1. Look through the psalm again. What words or phrases most strongly convey the spirit in which this psalm was written? Explain what each one communicates to you.

2. In verse 1 and 2, David refers to his failure as *transgression* (breaking through the boundaries of God's law), as *sin* (missing the mark of God's standard) and as *deceit*. Based on what you know of David's story (recorded in 2 Samuel 11—12), explain how the words describe different aspects of what David did.

3. What happens inwardly when we refuse to come clean with God (vv. 3-4)?

Why do you think David waited so long to admit and confess his sin?

4. According to verse 5, what is required to receive God's forgiveness?

5. What "waters" rise in your experience and seem to block God out (v. 6)?

6. David makes three declarations about the Lord in verse 7. Describe how God has recently met you in one of these ways.

7. What is David trying to communicate through his warning in verse 9?

8. How would you describe your normal response to God's forgiveness in your life?

9. How will this study of Psalm 32 enlarge and enhance your response when God graciously forgives you?

10. How does this psalm help you see God differently than you did before?

How will it help you see yourself differently?

Ask God to create a clean heart in you—a heart that rejoices over his forgiveness of your sin.

Now or Later

Compose a song or letter that expresses your joy in God's forgiveness. Sing, speak or dance the words in God's presence. If you are more reserved, carve out some quiet time to reflect on times when you have experienced God's forgiveness personally. Be sure to express with your lips the feelings you have in your heart about God's cleansing and full acceptance of you in Jesus, his Son.

---

*Corrie ten Boom's story is told in *The Hiding Place* (Minneapolis: World Wide Publishers, 1971), pp. 232-33.

5

Out of Debt!

The man sitting across the table from me moved between anger and tears. His brother (who was also his business partner) had brought the company to the verge of bankruptcy—for the third time! "He gets in trouble and starts siphoning off our money," my friend explained. "Then when we need the extra cash, it's gone."

The man's brother was a Christian. Every time his misuse of company funds was exposed, he admitted his wrong and begged for forgiveness. This time his wounded brother wasn't sure he had the strength to forgive him again.

GROUP DISCUSSION. What advice would you give this man?

PERSONAL REFLECTION. Who is the person you find easiest to forgive? Who is hardest for you to forgive?

When someone sins against us, that person is in our debt. They owe us something—an apology, compensation, restoration of what was lost. Jesus used the theme of debtors to teach his disciples a powerful lesson about forgiveness. *Read Matthew 18:21-35.*

---

1. Do you think Peter had a special reason for asking Jesus how often he was required to forgive the person who sins against him? Explain your answer.

---

2. The religious leaders of Jesus' day taught that three times was the limit on forgiveness. Peter thought he was being gracious to extend it to seven times. What does Jesus' answer tell you about how forgiveness operates in his kingdom?

---

3. What is your attitude when you are asked to forgive someone for the same offense three or four times? Explain why you have that attitude.

---

4. Does Jesus' command to forgive without limits mean that we are not to hold others accountable for what they do? Explain your answer.

5. When the king canceled the servant's enormous debt, the king took the loss himself. What insight does that give you about what it means for us to forgive others?

6. The comparison between the two debts in the parable is 600,000 to 1—the first servant was forgiven of a $600,000 debt and choked his fellow slave for one dollar! What does that show you about the first servant's attitude toward the king's mercy and grace?

7. The parable is obviously not about how to treat people who owe you money. What do the two debts represent in our lives?

What contrast does Jesus want us to draw?

8. If we refuse to forgive others, what happens in our lives (vv. 31-34)?

9. What does verse 35 mean? Does God forgive us only on the condition that we forgive others?

10. What person do you need to release from their debts to you?

11. How can you demonstrate God's mercy in a practical way to someone who has wronged you?

Thank God for forgiving your enormous debt of sin. Ask him to cultivate a forgiving spirit in you.

Now or Later

Sometimes the person we struggle to forgive is no longer in our lives or has died. If you or someone you know is facing that kind of unresolved situation, what specific things can you do that might bring a greater sense of peace?

6

When We Are Wounded

Matthew 18:15-20

He lives on the edge of my mind—a friend and former colleague who hurt me deeply. He makes his home several hundred miles away, but every so often he walks through the borders of my memory. I have to choose again to forgive him.

While I have refused to live in the bondage of bitterness toward this man, the relationship has never been reconciled. If I saw him on the street, I would not run up and put my arms around him. Some issues would have to be dealt with first.

GROUP DISCUSSION. How do you typically handle disagreements or conflicts with another person?

PERSONAL REFLECTION. Do you have an unresolved relationship in your past or present? What feelings surface when you think about that person?

Jesus took the matters of forgiveness and reconciliation very seriously. He was concerned enough to give us detailed instructions about how to confront people who wound us—and what to do if they refuse to admit they're wrong. This section of Jesus' teaching directly precedes the parable we read in study 5. *Read Matthew 18:15-20.*

1. Construct a simple flow chart of the steps and the possible responses outlined by Jesus in these verses.

What would it feel like to walk through this process as the one who was sinned against?

as the one who was sinning?

2. This process begins, "If your brother sins against you" (v. 15). Jesus' words apply directly to problems between "brothers" (Christians). What principles from these verses might help us resolve conflicts with non-Christians?

3. Why does Jesus place the burden of resolving the conflict on the offended person rather than on the offender?

4. What attitude do you think you should exhibit when you confront the person who has wounded you?

5. What are the benefits of taking two or three people with you the second time?

6. What will (hopefully) be accomplished by taking the extreme measures of verse 17?

7. What authority does Jesus give his followers and the church to act in such a way toward the person who refuses to repent (v. 18)?

8. What promises does Jesus make to those who are faithful in the areas of resolving conflict and pursuing reconciliation (vv. 19-20)?

9. What should you do if the offender never admits wrong?

How do you think God views that person?

---

10. What would be the results in your church or Christian fellowship if Jesus' instructions in this passage were followed?

What will be the result if we ignore or shortcut the process?

Ask God for the courage to go to those who sin against you—and the humility to go with grace.

Now or Later

The apostle Paul tells us that, when we stand before Jesus someday, all the hidden things will be revealed (1 Corinthians 4:5; 2 Corinthians 5:10). Perhaps the broken relationship we do not restore in this life will be dealt with in that future day. How will you feel if you have to confess guilt and admit wrong standing in Jesus' presence?

What steps can you take to begin to restore any broken relationship in your life? What person might be able to give you wise guidance in that process?

7

As We Forgive Others

When we pray for God's forgiveness, we are asking God to let us off the hook. Our request is that the burden of guilt resting on our shoulders would be lifted up and carried away. We want our relationship with the Father restored.

Receiving forgiveness is wonderful! Extending forgiveness is another matter. When we have been hurt, we want the one who hurt us to pay.

GROUP DISCUSSION. Complete the following excuses related to forgiveness from your own experience or from what you have heard others say.

I will forgive her when . . .
I should forgive them but . . .
I might forgive him if . . .

PERSONAL REFLECTION. Who from your past or present would you least want to meet today at the store or in an elevator? Why?

The Lord's Prayer contains many requests, from a plea for God's will to be carried out to a prayer for daily food. The fifth request in The Lord's Prayer is for forgiveness. "Forgive us our debts," we pray, "as we also have forgiven our debtors." *Read Matthew 6:5-15.*

---

1. What memories or impressions come to mind as you read the Lord's Prayer—memories from childhood or from worship experiences involving the prayer?

---

2. According to verses 5-8, what "games" do some people play with prayer?

---

3. What was Jesus trying to show us about our daily needs by incorporating a request for forgiveness in this model prayer?

---

4. Some readers of the prayer have concluded that God's forgiveness is *earned* by our own forgiveness of others. Other readers believe that our forgiveness of other people is the *evidence* that God has forgiven us. Explain why you agree or disagree with each view.

5. If we refuse to forgive another person, what do Jesus' words force us to conclude about ourselves (vv. 14-15)?

6. What reasons have you used (or could you use) to resist forgiving another person?

How would you counsel another Christian who came to you with those same reasons for not forgiving someone else?

7. Should forgiveness excuse the other person from the consequences of their actions? Explain your answer.

8. The final requests in the prayer are "lead us not into temptation, but deliver us from the evil one" (v. 13). What temptation from the evil one might we experience right after we pray for the courage to forgive someone?

9. Why does Jesus make forgiveness such a crucial issue for his followers?

10. What specific things can we as Christians do to demonstrate to our society that we are a forgiving community?

Pray the Lord's Prayer as your own prayer. Listen after each phrase to what God may be saying to you.

Now or Later

This study focuses on our forgiveness extended to others—but what if *you* are the one who needs to be forgiven? Think through your past and present to see if there are situations where you have hurt someone else. Work out a plan, and go to the individuals you have wronged. Admit your sin, and ask for forgiveness. The process will require courage and humility, but God will bring blessing to you through it.

8

Forgiving When We Don't Feel Like It

Philemon

The young Korean graduate student was mailing a letter home when a band of homeless teenagers attacked and beat him to death. The student's parents sat silently through the entire trial in Philadelphia. All they wanted was a chance to speak at the end.

After the guilty verdict was read, the parents knelt in a stunned courtroom and begged the judge to release their son's killers to them. They wanted to provide these boys with the love and care they had never experienced. The Korean couple told the judge that they were Christians, and they wanted to demonstrate the grace they had received from God to these boys who had wounded them so deeply.

The judge responded tearfully, "That is not the way our system of justice works."*

GROUP DISCUSSION. Did the Korean couple respond as Jesus would have, or were they misguided in their approach to the situation? Explain your position.

PERSONAL REFLECTION. What sin would you find it most difficult to forgive in your best friend? in your spouse? in your pastor? in your parents or child?

One of Paul's most personal letters was written to a rich man about one of his slaves. The slave Onesimus had stolen some money and run away from his owner, Philemon. When a runaway slave was caught, the customary punishment was branding—or worse. Somehow God brought Onesimus into contact with Paul—and the runaway slave came to faith in Jesus. Now Paul sends the slave back home to face his master. *Read Philemon.*

1. What can you glean from this letter about the circumstances Paul was in when he wrote it?

2. Based on verses 4-7 how would you describe Philemon to a Christian friend?

3. Why do you think Paul loved Onesimus so deeply (vv. 8-12)?

4. Onesimus had believed in Jesus. What change did his faith produce in the relationship between Onesimus and his owner, Philemon (vv. 15-16)?

5. Why doesn't Paul simply command Philemon to forgive Onesimus (vv. 8, 14, 17)?

6. Who would Paul plead with you to forgive if he wrote a letter to you today?

7. In what ways would Philemon be justified to refuse Paul's request that he accept Onesimus back into his household?

What risks did Onesimus take by going back to Philemon?

8. Paul asks Philemon to charge whatever Onesimus owes him

to Paul's account (vv. 18-19). How does Paul's request parallel
our forgiveness from Jesus?

9. What insight does Paul's request give you about the price
you may have to pay to forgive someone who has wronged
you?

10. In what ways does Philemon's restoration of Onesimus and
his acceptance of him as a brother parallel our acceptance by
God?

11. What does the story of Philemon and Onesimus teach us
about our acceptance of a person who has hurt us and who has
received our forgiveness?

What does it take to reestablish a sense of trust in someone
who has failed?

Ask the Lord to give you a heart to forgive the people who have hurt you most deeply.

Now or Later

An early church writer hints that there is more to this story than Paul's letter reveals. About forty years after Philemon was written, a Christian leader named Ignatius wrote a letter in which he greets the bishop of the region of Ephesus—a man named Onesimus. It's possible that, in time, Philemon freed Onesimus and that he eventually became the leading pastor in the region around Ephesus. Quite an accomplishment for a runaway slave!

What other notable Christians can you think of who came from a life of failure or rebellion to a place of great influence for God?

What person who has failed can you encourage in their faith?

---

*This story is told in Tony Campolo's book, *Wake Up, America* (Grand Rapids: Zondervan, 1991), pp. 47-48.

Leader's Notes

Leading a Bible discussion can be an enjoyable and rewarding experience. But it can also be *scary*—especially if you've never done it before. If this is your feeling, you're in good company. When God asked Moses to lead the Israelites out of Egypt, he replied, "O LORD, please send someone else to do it" (Ex 4:13). It was the same with Solomon, Jeremiah and Timothy, but God helped these people in spite of their weaknesses, and he will help you as well.

You don't need to be an expert on the Bible or a trained teacher to lead a Bible discussion. The idea behind these inductive studies is that the leader guides group members to discover for themselves what the Bible has to say. This method of learning will allow group members to remember much more of what is said than a lecture would.

These studies are designed to be led easily. As a matter of fact, the flow of questions through the passage from observation to interpretation to application is so natural that you may feel that the studies lead themselves. This study guide is also flexible. You can use it with a variety of groups—student, professional, neighborhood or church groups. Each study takes forty-five to sixty minutes in a group setting.

There are some important facts to know about group dynamics and encouraging discussion. The suggestions listed below should enable you to effectively and enjoyably fulfill your role as leader.

Preparing for the Study

1. Ask God to help you understand and apply the passage in your

own life. Unless this happens, you will not be prepared to lead others. Pray too for the various members of the group. Ask God to open your hearts to the message of his Word and motivate you to action.

2. Read the introduction to the entire guide to get an overview of the entire book and the issues which will be explored.

3. As you begin each study, read and reread the assigned Bible passage to familiarize yourself with it.

4. This study guide is based on the New International Version of the Bible. It will help you and the group if you use this translation as the basis for your study and discussion.

5. Carefully work through each question in the study. Spend time in meditation and reflection as you consider how to respond.

6. Write your thoughts and responses in the space provided in the study guide. This will help you to express your understanding of the passage clearly.

7. It might help to have a Bible dictionary handy. Use it to look up any unfamiliar words, names or places. (For additional help on how to study a passage, see chapter five of *How to Lead a LifeGuide Bible Study*, InterVarsity Press.)

8. Consider how you can apply the Scripture to your life. Remember that the group will follow your lead in responding to the studies. They will not go any deeper than you do.

9. Once you have finished your own study of the passage, familiarize yourself with the leader's notes for the study you are leading. These are designed to help you in several ways. First, they tell you the purpose the study guide author had in mind when writing the study. Take time to think through how the study questions work together to accomplish that purpose. Second, the notes provide you with additional background information or suggestions on group dynamics for various questions. This information can be useful when people have difficulty understanding or answering a question. Third, the leader's notes can alert you to potential problems you may encounter during the study.

10. If you wish to remind yourself of anything mentioned in the leader's notes, make a note to yourself below that question in the study.

Leading the Study

1. Begin the study on time. Open with prayer, asking God to help the group to understand and apply the passage.

2. Be sure that everyone in your group has a study guide. Encourage the group to prepare beforehand for each discussion by reading the introduction to the guide and by working through the questions in the study.

3. At the beginning of your first time together, explain that these studies are meant to be discussions, not lectures. Encourage the members of the group to participate. However, do not put pressure on those who may be hesitant to speak during the first few sessions. You may want to suggest the following guidelines to your group.

☐ Stick to the topic being discussed.

☐ Your responses should be based on the verses which are the focus of the discussion and not on outside authorities such as commentaries or speakers.

☐ These studies focus on a particular passage of Scripture. Only rarely should you refer to other portions of the Bible. This allows for everyone to participate in in-depth study on equal ground.

☐ Anything said in the group is considered confidential and will not be discussed outside the group unless specific permission is given to do so.

☐ We will listen attentively to each other and provide time for each person present to talk.

☐ We will pray for each other.

4. Have a group member read the introduction at the beginning of the discussion.

5. Every session begins with a group discussion question. The question or activity is meant to be used before the passage is read. The question introduces the theme of the study and encourages group members to begin to open up. Encourage as many members as possible to participate, and be ready to get the discussion going with your own response.

This section is designed to reveal where our thoughts or feelings need to be transformed by Scripture. That is why it is especially important not to read the passage before the discussion question is asked. The passage will tend to color the honest reactions people would otherwise give because they are, of course, supposed to think the way the Bible does.

You may want to supplement the group discussion question with an icebreaker to help people to get comfortable. See the community section of *Small Group Idea Book* for more ideas.

You also might want to use the personal reflection question with your group. Either allow a time of silence for people to respond individually or discuss it together.

6. Have a group member (or members if the passage is long) read aloud the passage to be studied. Then give people several minutes to read the passage again silently so that they can take it all in.

7. Question 1 will generally be an overview question designed to briefly survey the passage. Encourage the group to look at the whole passage, but try to avoid getting sidetracked by questions or issues that will be addressed later in the study.

8. As you ask the questions, keep in mind that they are designed to be used just as they are written. You may simply read them aloud. Or you may prefer to express them in your own words.

There may be times when it is appropriate to deviate from the study guide. For example, a question may have already been answered. If so, move on to the next question. Or someone may raise an important question not covered in the guide. Take time to discuss it, but try to keep the group from going off on tangents.

9. Avoid answering your own questions. If necessary, repeat or rephrase them until they are clearly understood. Or point out something you read in the leader's notes to clarify the context or meaning. An eager group quickly becomes passive and silent if they think the leader will do most of the talking.

10. Don't be afraid of silence. People may need time to think about the question before formulating their answers.

11. Don't be content with just one answer. Ask, "What do the rest of you think?" or "Anything else?" until several people have given answers to the question.

12. Acknowledge all contributions. Try to be affirming whenever possible. Never reject an answer. If it is clearly off-base, ask, "Which

verse led you to that conclusion?" or again, "What do the rest of you think?"

13. Don't expect every answer to be addressed to you, even though this will probably happen at first. As group members become more at ease, they will begin to truly interact with each other. This is one sign of healthy discussion.

14. Don't be afraid of controversy. It can be very stimulating. If you don't resolve an issue completely, don't be frustrated. Move on and keep it in mind for later. A subsequent study may solve the problem.

15. Periodically summarize what the group has said about the passage. This helps to draw together the various ideas mentioned and gives continuity to the study. But don't preach.

16. At the end of the Bible discussion you may want to allow group members a time of quiet to work on an idea under "Now or Later." Then discuss what you experienced. Or you may want to encourage group members to work on these ideas between meetings. Give an opportunity during the session for people to talk about what they are learning.

17. Conclude your time together with conversational prayer, adapting the prayer suggestion at the end of the study to your group. Ask for God's help in following through on the commitments you've made.

18. End on time.

Many more suggestions and helps are found in *How to Lead a LifeGuide Bible Study.*

Components of Small Groups

A healthy small group should do more than study the Bible. There are four components to consider as you structure your time together.

Nurture. Small groups help us to grow in our knowledge and love of God. Bible study is the key to making this happen and is the foundation of your small group.

Community. Small groups are a great place to develop deep friendships with other Christians. Allow time for informal interaction before and after each study. Plan activities and games that will help you get to know each other. Spend time having fun together—going on a picnic or cooking dinner together.

Worship and prayer. Your study will be enhanced by spending time praising God together in prayer or song. Pray for each other's needs—and keep track of how God is answering prayer in your group. Ask God to help you to apply what you are learning in your study.

Outreach. Reaching out to others can be a practical way of applying what you are learning, and it will keep your group from becoming self-focused. Host a series of evangelistic discussions for your friends or neighbors. Clean up the yard of an elderly friend. Serve at a soup kitchen together, or spend a day working on a Habitat house.

Many more suggestions and helps in each of these areas are found in *Small Group Idea Book.* Information on building a small group can be found in *Small Group Leaders' Handbook* and *The Big Book on Small Groups* (both from InterVarsity Press). Reading through one of these books would be worth your time.

Study 1. Our Forgiving Father. Luke 15:11-32.

Purpose: To explore the forgiving character of God and how we can respond to his grace.

General note. The parable of the prodigal son is the third in a cluster of three parables Jesus told. They were spoken in response to an accusation from the Pharisees (a strict group of Jews) that Jesus was getting too chummy with less-than-respectful people. A "sinner" according to the Pharisees was anyone who did not live in rigid observance of their laws and traditions. Jesus answered their accusation by pointing out God's intense search for those who are lost and separated from him and his explosive joy when one who was lost is found. The older brother in the third parable is actually a reflection of the Pharisees who objected to the lavishness of grace that Jesus extended to people who, in their eyes, were undeserving of God's attention.

Question 2. The purpose of this question is not to prompt detailed public rehearsal of past sins. Jesus spoke in very general terms as he described the younger son's wild living. Try to keep the responses focused on the various stages of the son's journey.

This parable is usually referred to as the parable of the prodigal son. The term *prodigal* (our term, not a term Jesus uses) actually refers to the young man's extravagant lifestyle in the distant country. He blew through his inheritance in a short time by reckless spending. We have come to use the term to refer to a person who lives for a while apart from the Lord and then returns in repentance. Jesus makes an interesting comparison in the parable between the boy who was prodigal in his spending and God who is prodigal—recklessly lavish—in his grace.

Question 3. The father could have forced the son to stay home by refusing to give him his inheritance, but the son would have served the father grudgingly. The father wanted a willing, joyful relationship with his son.

Question 4. The father waited for God to work in his son's heart. He knew that only God could bring the son to repentance. Searching for the son might have short-circuited that process. So he stayed at home but watched for the son with eager anticipation. The father believed that God would eventually bring the boy home.

Question 5. After exploring several options for the father's response, you might want to ask the group to identify which response they would have had to the runaway son.

Question 6. The father responded to the son with genuine affection, a return to his former status as son and heir (signified by the robe and the ring), and a joy-filled party. No lecture, no probation, no trip to the woodshed. Talk about how that response from God differs from the typical view of how God will act toward us when we return to him. Most people think God is waiting with a club!

Question 7. I'm sure the younger son served his father from that day on with grateful obedience. He didn't need a long list of rules or threats of discipline. He served his father obediently because he wanted to please the man who had been so gracious to him. When we realize how lavish God has been to us, we will want to live in a way that pleases him. A clear understanding of God's grace replaces all the rules and threats that others may want to use to keep us obedient to God.

Question 8. The older brother had served the father grudgingly, calculating what he would or should get from the deal. The father wanted the older son to see that his love was the same for both sons, but his joy at the return of the runaway was overwhelming. The older brother should have had the same joy but chose resentment instead.

Question 9. Christians who have grown up in the church (like the Pharisees to whom Jesus first spoke this parable) might begin to think that their obedience and good behavior have some merit with God. We have served God faithfully, and so we should get something from it. What "older-brother" Christians need to learn is that it took God's grace to save us too. Any obedient behavior in our lives should spring from the same sense of gratitude. Also, older-brother Christians can be grateful that they do not have to carry the scars and consequences of sinful rebellion in their lives that many prodigal Christians have to struggle with.

Question 10. Try to get the group to put what God would say to each of them in practical, personal terms. Challenge both prodigal and older-brother Christians to gain a new appreciation for the depth of God's grace.

Study 2. Why We Need Forgiveness. Ephesians 2:1-10.

Purpose: To help us comprehend our separation from God and what God has done to rescue us.

Question 1. Paul describes us as dead (unresponsive to God), as followers of the ways of the world and Satan, and as disobedient. We were sinful in our nature, and we confirmed that sinfulness by our actions. The picture Paul paints is that we were hopelessly separated from God by our sins.

Question 2. Human beings are separated from God by nature. We were conceived from parents who were fallen—the inheritance of all human beings from our original parents, Adam and Eve. We have confirmed that sinful nature by committing acts of sin. The truth is that *both* our sinful nature and our sinful deeds mark us out as sinners. But it is also as sinners that we qualify for God's grace.

Some members of your group may object that "innocent" babies, for example, cannot be sinners. The little child may not commit overt acts of sinful rebellion, but the capacity and inclination to sin is part of their innate human nature. It doesn't take long for that sinful nature to reveal itself in a child's attitude and behavior.

Question 3. God was prompted by his *love* to do something about humanity's desperate condition. He did not simply wait to "feel" like rescuing us; he acted on our behalf. In his *mercy*, God made it possible that we could escape the eternal consequences of our sin. In his *grace*, God gave us far more than we ever deserved by making us his own dear children.

Question 4. Forgiving someone else does not rest on our feelings but on a choice to act. In some cases we show mercy by not requiring the other person to suffer the consequences of their actions toward us. (Such as perhaps choosing not to report a theft to the police if the item is returned and the person is repentant.) In other cases they may need to make proper compensation. (For example, paying back a debt over time.) We show grace by restoring the person to a place of friendship with us.

Question 5. The person who believes in Jesus is made alive (responsive) to God. We are given new life; we are new creatures. The old nature is crucified with Christ, and we are made new. God sees us now not as disobedient sinners but as those who have been raised up with Christ and seated with Christ in the heavens.

Question 6. When we grasp the amazing grace and mercy of God, we are moved to new levels of gratitude and obedience to God. We have a desire to serve God—not in order to be saved but because we have been saved.

Question 7. No amount of effort or good works can atone for our sin. God is free to forgive because someone else has paid the penalty of our sin.

Question 8. The channel through which God's grace flows is faith—willing commitment to Jesus as Savior and Lord. Faith is not a "work"; it is the admission that I cannot atone for my own sin and that I trust in Christ alone to provide cleansing and reconciliation with God.

Question 9. God forgives those who recognize and admit that they are sinners. Forgiveness flows from us when the person who has hurt us acknowledges their sin. God comes to us with grace, the same gift we offer those who hurt us. We do not forgive because the other person "deserves" it. None of us deserve grace. That's what makes it grace!

Question 10. God acted to provide forgiveness before we were born. He displayed his love most fully in the sacrifice of his own Son. He has let us know that he will receive all who come to him through faith in Christ. We can assure others of our willingness to forgive by living a forgiving lifestyle. Other people see a grace-filled life in us and have confidence that they will receive grace even when they wound us. That isn't being a pushover or a doormat; that is being Christlike.

Study 3. Confessing Our Sin. 1 John 1:5—2:2.

Purpose: To come to a correct understanding of what genuine confession is and how it is linked to forgiveness.

Question 1. John's assertion that "God is light" is a reflection on the purity and transparency of God's character. God does not harbor any level of evil, deceit, untruth or falseness in his nature. Because God's nature is pure, every action that springs from God is pure and truthful.

Question 2. Christians are to walk in the realm of God's light. We are to be marked by the same purity and honesty. Our lives are to be transparent with nothing to conceal. Whatever is inconsistent with God's light is to be avoided and rejected. "To *walk in the light* means to shape one's whole being, all one's actions, decisions, thoughts and beliefs by the standard of the God who is light" (Marianne Meye Thompson, *1-3 John*, The IVP New Testament Commentary Series [Downers Grove: InterVarsity Press, 1992], p. 43).

Darkness is not simply sin or wrong. It is the realm that stands against God and is hostile to God. We are challenged to decide which circle we will live in—the realm of light or the realm of darkness.

Question 3. John saw that the Christian life was about making very clear choices—black or white, darkness or light, life or death. Claiming to have a relationship with God while continuing to walk in the realm that is hostile to God is a contradiction. A person's claim is backed up by lifestyle.

Question 4. Walking in the light does not imply sinlessness. Men and women who walk in the light do sin, but they also recognize the need to be purified from sin. As we walk in the realm of God's light, our sin and immaturity are exposed. God doesn't expose sin in order to condemn us; he exposes it to bring us to repentance and confession—to move us more clearly into the realm of his light. The provision for the purification of our hearts has already been provided in the atoning death of Jesus.

Question 5. Missing the mark of God's purity brings guilt—conviction from the Holy Spirit. Once the sin is confessed, God promises to forgive. The accusations and guilt that plague us after we have confessed come from Satan or from our own failure to claim God's promises. The solution to "false" guilt is not to keep begging God to forgive us but to stand firmly on God's promise that he has forgiven us.

Question 6. John was writing about some people who claimed that, since God is light, his children share God's state of absolute purity. They concluded that since they were born of God, they had entered a level of sinlessness that required nothing more of them. John does desire that believers live without sin (2:1), but he refutes the idea that we lose the capacity to sin.

Question 7. Confession is not just saying, "I'm sorry." It is naming the wrong and taking full responsibility for the action. Once we admit our sin and own it, God promises to forgive us. The penalty has already been paid by the death of Jesus. The benefits of Jesus' death are applied to us, and we are under no further obligation. Confession also implies a turning toward God with a greater desire to conform more closely to his character.

Question 8. God anchors his promise of forgiveness to his own unchangeable character. We won't catch God in a bad mood, and he won't decide someday to stop forgiving. Continuing to sin against him in the same way may grieve God's heart and may prompt his loving discipline in our lives, but he is consistently faithful to forgive.

Question 9. When we admit our sin, Jesus "speaks with the Father in our defense." That doesn't mean that the Father is hard-hearted or reluctant to forgive us. John's words are designed to give us confidence to come to God in confession because we know that Jesus will intercede for us. Such unity exists between the Father and the Son that God will grant whatever Jesus asks for. What he asks for us is forgiveness—and the Father graciously grants it.

Question 10. These current-day "errors" are similar to the errors that

John exposes in this passage. God's grace is never a license to sin. True confession makes us want to be more like God. Genuine salvation is revealed in a desire to walk in the light. On the other hand, Jesus' sacrifice on the cross was sufficient to cover all our sin. God's grace and forgiveness are bound only by the extent of Jesus' atoning sacrifice, not the size of our sin.

Study 4. The Shout of a Forgiven Man. Psalm 32.
Purpose: To learn to express our joy for God's gracious forgiveness.
Question 1. Words like *blessed, songs of deliverance, rejoice, glad* and *sing* convey the sense of relief and happiness David felt as he contemplated God's amazing forgiveness and love of him. The goal of this study is to translate that same spirit of joy into our experience as we consider God's forgiveness of us.
Question 2. The story of David's sin and repentance is recorded in 2 Samuel 11—12. As the group leader, you may want to read through the account as background for this study. Psalm 51, David's psalm of confession, gives additional insight.

The seventh commandment instructs God's people not to commit adultery; the sixth commandment prohibits murder. David clearly "transgressed" both aspects of God's law. Furthermore, God requires his people to live holy lives. David, as king, was to be a model to his people of a man committed to doing God's will. David dramatically "missed the mark" of God's desire for his life. Finally, David tried to hide his sin with a series of cover-ups and secret plots. God, however, saw it all.
Question 3. David's testimony is that, as long as he tried to hide his sin, he dried up inwardly. He found no joy in worship or in God's Word. His spirit began to shrivel. David acknowledged that it was God's hand that produced this inner dryness. God did not discipline David out of anger but out of love. He used David's inward anguish to bring him to the place of obedience and restoration. David came out of the experience a changed man.
Question 4. God looks for (1) an honest, transparent admission of sin, (2) a willingness to stop excusing or justifying our sin and (3) a willing confession to the Lord of the wrong we have done.

Question 5. We usually think of difficult experiences as the "waters" that hinder our sense of God's love or God's care. David makes it clear that our own disobedience may cloud our perception of God too. Like a loving father who allows a wandering child to feel "lost" so the child will learn to stay close, God may allow us to feel like he is far away so we will turn back to him in repentance. God, of course (like the loving father), never allows the child to wander out of his sight or beyond the reach of his grace.

Question 6. Allow members of the group to express how God has touched their lives in a personal way. Each person should be given an opportunity to tell their story without judgment from others in the group.

Question 7. David does not want us to be so stubborn that God has to bring us to a place of brokenness in order to get us to repent. We are challenged to confess our sin willingly and quickly.

Question 8. Unfortunately, many Christians view God's forgiveness as a right not as a gracious gift. We just expect and assume that God will forgive, instead of appreciating the wonder of God's grace.

Question 9. This psalm should prompt a greater spirit of joy and gratitude to God for his abundant forgiveness to us. We give God praise because he cleansed us at salvation; we should also bless him for his willingness to forgive us day after day.

Question 10. Some people see God sitting in heaven ready to club us if we step out of line. Sin certainly grieves God, and he may use drastic measures at times to bring us to repentance. When we confess our sin, however, he is anxious to forgive and to restore us to the place of fellowship with him.

The psalm also helps us see that we don't have to live under a burden of guilt. Once God has forgiven us, we are cleansed. We may still have to suffer the consequences of our sin (as David did), but we can face those consequences knowing that our hearts are clean before God.

Study 5. Out of Debt! Matthew 18:21-35.

Purpose: To see God's forgiveness of us as the backdrop for our forgiveness of others.

Group discussion. Read (or ask a group member to read) the opening paragraphs, and then pose the discussion question to the group. Allow some debate or discussion, but don't let it go too far. Try to get everyone to add his or her opinion. Before moving to question 1, you may want to ask the group to think about the personal reflection question. Public answers probably aren't appropriate, but each person can reflect on the question in his or her own mind.

Question 1. Peter is probably responding to the instruction Jesus gave about forgiveness in verses 15-20. He may also have had a particular person in mind who he had already forgiven several times—"Let's see, have I forgiven Andrew four times, or is it five?"

Question 2. Jesus wanted his followers to understand that there are no limits on forgiveness. Living under God's reign means we don't keep track of how many times we have forgiven someone else. Some versions read "seventy times seven"; other versions read "seventy-seven times." The Greek text of the Gospel can be read either way—and either way, the point is the same. Forgiveness is unlimited. Forgiveness is not a matter of calculation but a way of life.

Question 4. Jesus is not saying that we forgive without expecting change or without holding others accountable. The abusive husband or the rebellious child can be forgiven, but they can also be called to demonstrate a changed life. In some cases the most loving thing may be to remove ourselves from the life of a person who cannot behave correctly.

Question 5. Forgiveness involves accepting the loss and pain ourselves. The king absorbed the slave's debt; we absorb the pain of another person's sin against us and place them under no further obligation.

Question 6. A talent was a huge sum of money, equal to the average worker's salary for twenty years. A denarius was the average pay for one day's work. The first servant's experience of forgiveness obviously had not instilled in him any sense of gratitude or humility.

Question 7. The enormous debt to the king represents our debt of sin to God. The smaller debt from the servant represents the debt of those who hurt or wound us. Jesus is not minimizing the pain we feel from others. He is just trying to demonstrate dramatically the relative size of the two debts.

Question 8. A lack of forgiveness puts us in a "prison" of anger, revenge, bitterness and disobedience. Our "tormentors" work at driving us deeper and deeper into despair and hatred. Just like the servant could never repay the debt to the king, the torment that emerges from an unforgiving spirit never ends.

Question 9. God the Judge will do to the unforgiving person exactly what he or she has done to others. God is a source of wonderful mercy and grace, but a refusal on our part to forgive others is evidence that we have never truly received the forgiveness of God.

Michael Wilkins expands on this "core" of the parable: "A person who has not experienced God's grace and mercy will not experience his forgiveness. He will, like the first servant, accept the personal benefits, but it will be only superficial. It will not penetrate a hard and wicked heart to produce transformation. Such a person will thus experience eternal condemnation" ("Matthew," in *The NIV Application Commentary* [Grand Rapids: Zondervan, 2004], p. 625). A forgiven heart produces the fruit of forgiveness.

Study 6. When We Are Wounded. Matthew 18:15-20.

Purpose: To understand and obey Jesus' directives for dealing with those who sin against us.

Group discussion. Let group members respond to this question without judgment from you or from others. The goal is to get people to think about how they handle conflict, not to evaluate their approach.

Question 1. Have a large white board or poster board to set up so you can write down the steps and possible responses as the group points them out. Make it a team project to construct the chart. A suggested flow chart is available at the IVP website under the name of this study guide.

Question 2. Jesus clearly limits the discussion to offenses between Christians. The key to resolving conflicts with unbelievers is found in the book of Hebrews: "Make every effort to live in peace with all men" (12:14). We can apply some of Jesus' principle, however, to our relationships with non-Christians—approaching the person privately rather than publicly, going to them in humility rather than anger, seeking the help of a mutual friend, if necessary, to promote reconciliation.

Question 3. Our natural tendency is to sit and wait for the other person to apologize. Meanwhile, the other person may not know they have hurt us or may not care. The wounded person is the one motivated to confront the issue and restore the relationship.

Question 4. Our attitude is a vital part of the restoration process. If we go with the purpose of attacking or condemning the other person, we will just make the situation worse. Paul, in Galatians 6:1-2, suggests that we go to a sinning brother or sister with humility, recognizing our own capacity for the same sin or even worse sin.

Question 5. If the other person will not admit his or her wrong and reconcile with you privately, witnesses are taken to verify to the church (if it progresses to that point) that every attempt was made to resolve the issue. The presence of other Christians may also help to persuade the offender to deal correctly with sin.

Question 6. The goal of the whole process is not to push the offender away but to draw him back into a proper relationship with the Lord and with other believers. If the offender refuses to repent, the Christian community gets involved to demonstrate a form of "tough love." The offender is excluded in an attempt to get him or her to admit wrongdoing and to be restored to full fellowship.

Question 7. Jesus was declaring that, if a believer and/or the church act according to the steps he set down, they can be assured that God ("heaven") is in agreement with their actions.

Question 8. Repentance and reconciliation open our hearts to greater obedience and greater spiritual privilege. Christians who obey Christ in these difficult areas of confession and forgiveness will find the spiritual boundaries of their lives expanded.

Question 9. Lack of repentance is never an excuse to refuse to forgive the offender. We can still forgive the person and move beyond bitterness or revenge. The relationship will not be restored until the offender repents, but we can go on in our walk with the Lord in freedom and joy.

Question 10. Shortcutting the process is not helpful for anyone! The offender is never forced to face his wrong; the offended person is tempted to live with bitterness and anger; the Lord is grieved by our lack of obedience and courage.

Study 7. As We Forgive Others. Matthew 6:5-15.

Purpose: To motivate us to incorporate our need of forgiveness and our responsibility to forgive into our daily prayer life.

General note. What we call "the Lord's Prayer" is more accurately called "the disciples prayer" because Jesus offered it as a model for our prayer life. Jesus was sinless, so he never had to ask for forgiveness. I have written a LifeGuide on the Lord's Prayer that explores each phrase of this much-loved passage.

Question 2. Jesus warns us against praying just for applause or to trumpet our piety. He also reminds us that God is not impressed with the empty repetition of prayers. God looks at the heart of the person who prays.

Question 3. Our need for forgiveness is daily. That doesn't mean that we sin continually, but everyday we need to be aware of our capacity for sin. Allowing God to search our lives and hearts, as well as being ready to confess whatever he exposes that does not please him, is part of living a "Lord's Prayer lifestyle".

Question 4. We know from other passages of Scripture that God's forgiveness is given to us freely in response to faith in Christ (Acts 10:43) and confession of sin (1 Jn 1:9). What Jesus seems to emphasize is that the *evidence* of God's forgiveness in our lives is that we are quick to forgive others. Forgiving another person is the outflow of God's grace to us.

Question 5. Continuing in our refusal to forgive someone after God has prompted us by his Word and by his Spirit to forgive reveals that we have not experienced God's forgiveness—or that we do not comprehend the depth of God's forgiveness and grace to us.

Question 6. The purpose of this question is to get the group to think through appropriate responses to the common excuses for refusing to forgive: he hurt me too deeply; she hasn't said she is sorry; I will forgive when he changes. Does God say that to us when we come to him for forgiveness? Probe how to respond to each excuse in a practical and biblical way. Be sensitive to the fact that a person's excuse may be the very issue they are struggling with personally.

Question 7. Forgiveness does not mean that consequences should not follow. When Jesus was crucified, he asked his Father to forgive those who had rejected him. That doesn't mean their guilt and responsibility were wiped away. The apostle Peter later said to the same people that they were responsible for putting Jesus to death (Acts 2:23). Jesus' prayer was answered when God gave those he prayed for the opportunity to be forgiven by faith in the very person they had crucified. You may forgive the person who robs you on the street, but that person should still face the consequences of his action under the law.

Question 8. We may be tempted to delay forgiveness or refuse forgiveness. Satan may implant ideas of revenge or encourage a spirit of bitterness in our hearts. Even other people may try to divert us from making the difficult choices to obey God.

Question 9. Jesus knew that the unbelieving world would not be changed by a new system of doctrine or a new organization for religious observance. What would change the world was a group of people who could live together in genuine forgiveness and love.

Study 8. Forgiving When We Don't Feel Like It. Philemon.
Purpose: To explore how we can genuinely forgive the people who have hurt us most deeply.

Question 1. The letter to Philemon (fi-**lee**-mon) was written during Paul's first imprisonment in Rome. Acts 28:16, 30-31 says that, while Paul waited for a hearing before Caesar, he was under house arrest in Rome and received friends freely. Paul calls himself an old man (v. 9) and a prisoner of Jesus Christ (vv. 1, 9).

Question 2. Philemon was a Christian and was wealthy enough to own slaves. He lived in Colossae, a city near Ephesus in Asia Minor. Perhaps Paul had led Philemon to faith in Christ since, in verse 19, Paul says Philemon owed Paul his very self (or his own soul). Philemon was a man of faith, love, active witness for Christ and generosity toward Paul and others.

Onesimus (oh-**ness**-i-mus) had run away from Philemon's household and had made his way to Rome to get lost in the masses of runaways crowding the capital city. Under God's direction Onesimus came in contact with Paul who reached out to him in grace and mercy. Perhaps Paul even recognized the slave from the time Paul had spent in the area of Ephesus and with the Christians at Colossae.

Question 3. Onesimus had obviously come to faith in Christ under Paul's ministry. The slave became Paul's "son" while Paul was in prison (v. 10). The Greek name *Onesimus* means "useful." The name was originally given to Onesimus either in mockery or in anticipation of his usefulness as a slave. Onesimus proved useless to Philemon by stealing from him and running away. Now Paul is returning Onesimus to Philemon with the testimony that the slave had been useful to Paul (v. 11) and had served Paul in Philemon's place (v. 13).

Question 4. Onesimus was now a "dear brother" in the Lord to both Paul and Philemon. Paul never ordered or encouraged believers to free their slaves. He just reminded them that believing slaves were brothers and sisters in the Lord. Eventually Christian masters could no longer in good conscience hold their fellow believers in slavery.

Question 5. Paul could have leveraged his relationship with Philemon or used his authority as an apostle to require Philemon to accept and forgive Onesimus. Paul's desire, however, was that Philemon would respond willingly to his request. A willing response would also assure Paul that Philemon had genuinely forgiven Onesimus and that he wasn't carrying a secret grudge against him.

Question 7. Running away as a slave was a serious crime. Sixty million slaves populated the Roman Empire, and the Roman economy was dependent on their work power. When a runaway was caught, the slave was usually branded on the forehead with an "F" (for *fugitive*). Sometimes masters tortured or mutilated a runaway slave. Under Roman law a master could execute a runaway slave without consequence.

Onesimus' return to Philemon's household without punishment could have sparked attempts by other slaves to run away. Furthermore, Philemon would have had a difficult time trusting Onesimus after he had betrayed him once.

On the other hand, Onesimus risked physical punishment by returning. He could have been sold to another master. Runaway slaves were sometimes condemned to be gladiators and forced to fight to the death in Roman arenas.

Question 8. We are guilty of sin before God and deserve the maximum penalty (Eph 2:1-5; Rom 6:23). But Jesus paid the penalty of our sin on the cross, and now he can intervene on our behalf with the Father. The penalty we deserve is placed on Christ's account—an account already paid in full. Paul had to appeal to Philemon's love for Paul; Jesus appeals to the completed sacrifice on the cross.

Question 9. Forgiving others requires a willingness to absorb the hurt and loss ourselves. Forgiveness is a promise that we won't keep bringing up the offense in our relationship with the other person. It also means we won't harbor resentment or carry a grudge in our own hearts.

Question 10. God not only forgives our sin but also makes us his own dear children. Philemon did not simply return Onesimus to his former place as a slave in the household, he also began to regard him as a brother. He sat next to him in church!

Question 11. Since we cannot know a person's intentions fully (as God can), full reconciliation sometimes requires a period of demonstrated faithfulness. It is not a lack of forgiveness to ask for the evidence of a changed life in those we forgive. Philemon had the evidence of Onesimus' changed life from the observation of Paul. Our goal is not to hope those we forgive will fail but to encourage them toward continued obedience to God.

Douglas Connelly is a pastor, writer and speaker who lives in Davison, Michigan. He has written seventeen LifeGuide® Bible Studies as well as several books, including The Bible for Blockheads *and* Angels Around Us. *He and his wife, Karen, have three children and six grandchildren.*

What Should We Study Next?

A good place to continue your study of Scripture would be with a book study. Many groups begin with a Gospel such as *Mark* (20 studies by Jim Hoover) or *John* (26 studies by Douglas Connelly). These guides are divided into two parts so that if twenty or twenty-six weeks seems like too much to do at once, the group can feel free to do half and take a break with another topic. Later you might want to come back to it. You might prefer to try a shorter letter. *Philippians* (9 studies by Donald Baker), *Ephesians* (11 studies by Andrew T. and Phyllis J. Le Peau) and *1 & 2 Timothy and Titus* (11 studies by Pete Sommer) are good options. If you want to vary your reading with an Old Testament book, consider *Ecclesiastes* (12 studies by Bill and Teresa Syrios) for a challenging and exciting study.

There are a number of interesting topical LifeGuide studies as well. Here are some options for filling three or four quarters of a year:

Basic Discipleship
Christian Beliefs, 12 studies by Stephen D. Eyre
Christian Character, 12 studies by Andrea Sterk & Peter Scazzero
Christian Disciplines, 12 studies by Andrea Sterk & Peter Scazzero
Evangelism, 12 studies by Rebecca Pippert & Ruth Siemens

Building Community
Fruit of the Spirit, 9 studies by Hazel Offner
Spiritual Gifts, 8 studies by R. Paul Stevens
Christian Community, 10 studies by Rob Suggs

Character Studies
David, 12 studies by Jack Kuhatschek
New Testament Characters, 10 studies by Carolyn Nystrom
Old Testament Characters, 12 studies by Peter Scazzero
Women of the Old Testament, 12 studies by Gladys Hunt

The Trinity
Meeting God, 12 studies by J. I. Packer
Meeting Jesus, 13 studies by Leighton Ford
Meeting the Spirit, 10 studies by Douglas Connelly

Other LifeGuide® Bible Studies by Douglas Connelly

Angels
Daniel
Elijah
Encountering Jesus
Following Jesus
Good & Evil
Heaven
Heroes of Faith
I AM
John
The Lord's Prayer
Meeting the Spirit
The Messiah
Miracles
Names of God
The Twelve Disciples